Alice Barber is a psychotherapist who treats emotionally troubled young children in their homes, schools and in her office. In this book she thoughtfully, lucidly and with great sensitivity, invites us to join her in trying to understand the disturbing, sometimes terrifying relational narratives her clients persuade her to (re)enact with them. In the course of presenting their narratives, she also discusses, with impressive self-awareness, how treating children shapes and reshapes her image of herself both as a therapist and as a person. In over sixty years as a therapist and teacher of clinical practice, I've never read a book on child treatment that I found more illuminating, or for that matter, more enjoyable. It's a "must read" for anyone seriously interested in understanding how children experience the caretaking adults in their lives, and how they communicate with their therapists.

Gerald Schamess
Professor Emeritus, Smith College School for Social Work

Alice Barber's book brings clinical work with children alive in stunning stories that show how truths emerge in sudden and unexpected ways. In this book we are in the presence of astute clinical listening that is rare in a world driven by evidence-based practices. Invited to witness uncharted, unexpected, nuanced moments that happen between child and therapist, we get a glimpse of effects that reach far beyond a moment. This book is a vital resource for anyone interested in clinical work with children, or for that matter, anyone interested in truly listening to children.

Annie G. Rogers, Ph.D
Professor of Psychoanalysis and Clinical Psychology,
Hampshire College. Author of *A Shining Affliction* and
The Unsayable

This book is a love letter to child therapy, reminding both new and seasoned therapists of the richness of staying in the moment, feeling deeply, and listening hard to the stories that children tell us."

Martha B. Straus, Ph.D
Professor of Clinical Psychology at Antioch University
New England. Author of *No-Talk Therapy for Children* and
Adolescents and Adolescent Girls in Crisis: Intervention and Hope

In these tenderly crafted vignettes of her therapeutic work with children, Alice Barber opens herself fully to each child's sorrow and horror, taking the reader along for moments of surprise, poignant connection, and yes, hilarity. This book gives voice to the emotional and sometimes unruly inner life of a therapist extraordinarily gifted at working with children in pain. Blue Butterfly Open is a stirring and memorable work.

Cynthia Monahon, Psy.D
Founder, The Children's Clinic, Northampton, Massachusetts
Author of *Children and Trauma: A Guide for Parents
and Professionals*

This book is a joy to read —graceful, moving, and at times devastating— revealing the true nature of how healing can happen in human relationships. Alice Barber illuminates tender, incandescent moments of connection between herself and the children who come to her in pain. A testimony to her skill as both therapist and writer, Blue Butterfly Open *invites readers to share in the elusive poignancy of earning the trust of a child.*

SuEllen Hamkins, M.D.
Author of *The Art of Narrative Psychiatry*

Written with grace and humor, empathy and compassion, Barber takes the reader on a remarkable journey into the heart and mind of a therapist who seeks to help troubled children. Each chapter highlights a shared moment of vulnerability between them, seemingly small in scope, but rare and profound in its meanings for both child and therapist. Readers will be moved and sometimes amused as Barber reveals her own understandings, feelings, questions, and rebellions against the conventional wisdoms of her field—as when she sits though six sessions with a boy who curls up in his chair and goes to sleep 'because it is what he needed to do.' Passionate and wise, she gives eloquent testimony to her deep belief in the collaborative nature of healing.

Joan Cenedella, Ed.D
Educator/Administrator, Bank Street College
of Education 1970–1996
Author of *Nothing Brave Here*

This eloquent and poetic book reveals the enormous potential for transformation that is possible in child psychotherapy. Master therapist Alice Barber's willingness to reflect on her own fears, sorrows and joys allows us to enter with her the difficult terrain of childhood trauma and emerge with valuable wisdom.

Barbara Weiner Dubeck, M.Ed, LMHC, LCSW
Founding Director, The Garden: A Center for Grieving
Children and Teens

BLUE
BUTTERFLY
OPEN

BLUE BUTTERFLY OPEN

Moments From a Child Psychotherapy Practice

Alice Barber

GALLERY *of*
READERS PRESS

NORTHAMPTON, MASSACHUSETTS

Gallery of Readers Press
16 Vernon Street,
Northampton, MA 01060

A 501(c)3 organization, Gallery of Readers Press thanks the
individuals whose generosity makes the publication of this volume
possible, in particular our board members and donors. For more
information about Gallery of Readers or to make a tax deductible
donation, please contact us at galleryofreaders.org.

Book designed by James McDonald
The Impress Group, Northampton, Massachusetts
jamesmcdonaldbooks.com

Front cover art by Dakota Joseph
Author photo by Meryl Cohn

ISBN: 978-1-4951-6900-7

Dedicated to Bonnie and Jesse Sky, my loves

CONTENTS

Dear Reader,

There are many types of blue butterflies. Ours is specifically the Blue Morpho as shown in a photograph taken by a little boy and then delivered to me without my having asked him for it. He had captured and given me the rarest of sights, a blue butterfly, open, resting on a leaf. That blue butterfly has become for me a symbol of brief moments of truth in the relationship between therapist and child. Moments the therapist can recognize as they are happening, and others that flit by, recognized only in retrospect. This book is about those moments.

Blue Butterfly Open is not a "how-to" of child psychotherapy. These essays are not case studies in the traditional sense. For example, they do not begin with "Client presented for therapy due to an ongoing struggle with behavior at home and at school." In some of these stories, you may not know a developmental history, a diagnosis, or a score on any type of behavioral rating scale. You will not know if I engaged in an evidence-based practice of some sort, nor will you know the course of treatment. You may not even know why the child is in therapy in the first place.

I am not suggesting that, should you find yourself doing therapy with a young child, you do as I have done. Nor am I suggesting to those of you who are not in the field of child psychotherapy that these stories are typical of what all sessions are like. What I hope you will know after reading this book is that, in a therapeutic relationship between child and therapist, there are moments of vulnerability on both sides; the relationship depends on this. Sometimes, both people in the therapy room are trembling or crying or laughing. And that is okay.

If you are a therapist for young children, I hope this book will help you be brave. I hope it will help you remember that there are times in which you know nothing. That these times of knowing nothing, these times of trusting your gut feelings, the connections you make with your clients, and some faraway graduate school training are the times in which beautiful, open moments with children can be born. I do not wish to imply that "not knowing" means "no road map" or "no direction." Quite the contrary. It means being bold enough to let the true direction of treatment emerge as you are led by your client, no matter how young. It takes skill and self-acceptance to bring a "not knowing" stance to a therapy relationship. Therapists are not the "fixers" of children. Therapists are the holders of moments.

The Blue Morpho butterfly can be called Common Morpho, the Emperor, or *Morpho peleides*. It is iridescent. The blue on the inside of the wings is caused by the diffraction of light from its tiny scales. The outside of the wings is not blue, but brown, with owl eyes along the edges, like an edging of lace, sewn on in meticulous fashion. This butterfly enjoys meals of mango and kiwi, and it uses the speed by which it flutters its wings and flashes its colors to ward off predators.

My earlier attempts at taking just the photo this boy later gave to me had failed miserably. More on this soon. I'd run after these butterflies, hid from them, tried to fool them, bribed them, and prayed. But the wings always closed up much too quickly for the agility of my thumb on shutter release. The result was blurred streaks or absolutely nothing at all, empty space, an opportunity missed. I am astonished that the boy gave me this particular photo. To remind me of my astonishment, I have given it a permanent home on the bulletin board in my office so that whenever I notice it I can remember my appreciation for these moments of sublime connection.

I am deeply grateful to this boy and to each of the children and their loved ones who allowed me to include their stories here. While identifying information has been changed and dialogue from the sessions has been slightly altered, my intention is to relay the essential truth of our exchanges.

—Alice Barber

Swimming

Isn't swimming what I do? Each and every therapy session, with each and every child, it feels like I'm swimming. I dive in and maneuver through the perils of seaweed, shipwrecks, and electric eels. Yes, I think it is exactly what I do.

On a good day you might mistake me for Esther Williams. My toes are pointed, my hair is curled into ringlets (even in the water!), and my smile is sparkling. I don't break a sweat or pant like a dog. Instead, I beautifully execute some obscure theory of the human psyche. At other times, I can be seen in a limp dead man's float or sputtering out water that has made its way into my nostrils without invitation. At the end of these weeks, I collect my paycheck and go home.

At times, I am graceful. At times, I am in need of a lifeguard. Mostly, I am swimming a predictable crawl stroke with a breath on every second circle of my right arm, keeping time to some old song in my head, noticing the familiar marks on the bottom of the pool. It is the kind of stroke I see old men do in the slow lane at the Y on Friday evenings.

One day, unexpectedly, I took an actual swim with one of my child clients. This swim was no predictable crawl. It was a butterfly stroke with grand wingspan and swift dolphin kicks. This was in real water, not simply in the murk of imagination, memory, and fantasy. We were in a pool of average size and somewhat below-average temperature. It was unexpected because it was not what I planned, or how I thought things should go, until I was there.

It was summer and it was hot. Several weeks earlier in that season of heat waves, fireworks, and the buzzing of cicadas, the six-year-old girl was removed from the home she shared with her biological parents. That's how we say it in this field. The child was removed by authorities and placed in foster care. Removed and Placed. Removed and Placed. The details of "Removed" and the intricacies of "Placed" are lost in translation. They are lost in the actions of a mother and father who did not do what they most needed to do. They are lost in the details of drug abuse and violence and an early childhood usurped by chaos.

This vocabulary perhaps helps us in some way. It keeps us a certain number of inches, feet, or miles away from the horror of what is happening. As if such language could shield us from the horror of the treatment of the child. Or the horror of the walk from the family's front door and into the car of a stranger. Or the horror of the fact that it is never the parents we remove, taking them from their homes, their bedrooms, their neighborhoods in the middle of the night. It is the horror of the removal, the breaking point, the breaking apart. Sometimes it is the actual pulling of arms from arms, peeling hands from hands, and the screaming on both sides.

"Phew," we like to say to ourselves in this field, "at least she isn't still in this or that awful situation." But we think very little about the pulling away of a child from a parent. That exact moment. Regardless of circumstances, children love their parents.

On my way to see her, this girl who I had seen weekly for the past year prior to her recent removal from her parents, I analyze the word "remove." Re-move. Remove: 1. To change position. 2. A degree of remoteness or separation. To change position *again*, I think. Re-run, re-do, resume.

When I arrive, the girl stands on the edge of a dark

wooden deck by the pool. She's sopping wet and in a pink bathing suit. I take in the Disney princess, fair-skinned and smiling, on the front of the suit. It looks like a hand-me-down or castoff. It sags around her bottom and wrinkles around her middle. The girl wears an oversized snorkel mask, a little foggy. I am reminded of getting my first pair of glasses in fourth grade and worrying that they made me look like an owl.

As I place my workbags down by the side of a chair, the girl raises her hands. Her fingers are puckered and pale.

"No more questions!" She yells this with pinched nose and jumps into the pool. Water splashes back up onto the deck. I jump out of its way. She squats on the bottom of the pool like a small pink frog. Her hair encircles her head, much like that of the princess on her front.

Her foster mom greets me near the back door of the house.

"Lawyers have been here, and another officer. They've been asking her all sorts of things," she says. I nod. I wait for the girl to emerge from the water. Bubbles rise from her mouth, and she moves upward.

"No more questions!" She is louder this time.

"I'm not going to ask any questions!" I am emphatic, but she is already back down. I am not going to ask questions like the others, I think. I never have. That's not the way I do it.

I watch her there, underwater. I suppose I could call out to her. Order her to dry off, to join me for our 50-minute hour. But it seems that a dry, by-the-book session is not where she is. She is living free from the voices and the demands of others, where everything is muffled and soft. Smarty.

I take off my sandals and jump in the pool next to her.

I like now to think, in the retelling, that I jumped in with abandon. That it had been that easy. My entry was actually much more methodical. I'm not generally a spontaneous person. I am a picky eater and a follower of routines. I cry upon being stopped by police for driving over the speed limit, and I iron my clothes. I generally avoid cold, wet circumstances. I actually made my way into her pool inch by agonizing inch, with associated grimaces and sharp intakes of breath. Thankfully, she was my last appointment of the day.

In the water, my jeans feel heavy and weigh me down. I'm reminded of a lifesaving course where I had to make a flotation device from a pair of jeans. My denim shirt sucks at my skin. The water is cold. I squat on the bottom like a frog. We both come up for air.

"No more questions," I say to the girl in the too-big bathing suit.

She swims away. I stay where I am. Her snorkel mask is still foggy. Her nose is running, two long spider web lines. She splashes her hands then, in the water, whips her feet this way and that.

"Alice, help me!" She goes under and comes back up. I wonder if this is real. Is she drowning? Should I even be in here?

"My boat is sinking! I need help!" She splashes again, gulps down water, spits some of it back out. "All of the other boats are sinking, too! Except for your boat, Alice, all of the others are sinking!!!"

I swim to where she is; water splashes into my eyes. I grab hold of her slippery arm and think back to graduate school: *Rule 1: Don't ever touch your clients.* We were given this message in a variety of ways.

"Look at all of the other boats, Alice! You have to save me!"

I look around, as if with a telescope. "I see the other boats sinking," I say, and take hold of her other arm.

"I have a good hold on you right now . . . I've got you for now." I wonder if I sound enough like a captain.

"Iceberg ahead!" I want to say, but don't.

The girl looks frightened. "Oh no! Alice, we are both sinking now!!!"

We move again to the bottom of the pool, together. I open my eyes under water and see that she is looking at me through her mask. Her hair floats around her head. She smiles. I grip her under her arms and pull her to the surface. I lift her up above my head toward the sky. She drips onto my face. I look at her.

"No more questions," I say. Her body is limp.

"You're beautiful," she says.

My breath catches.

And then, with the might of her being, she kicks me squarely in my belly, my softest place. For a moment, my wind is gone and I am speechless. Which is what she may have wanted in the first place. I drop her and double over. She wiggles her body away from where I stand and swims to the other side. Her foster mother stands by the side of the pool with a towel in her hand and waits for us to get out and dry off.

Moo

A boy of five walks into my office and, without hesitation or consultation, begins to pull everything that rests at edges of the room about a foot and a half in toward the middle. I allow him to redecorate in this way. I let him lead me to where he needs to in the mountains of heights and the pockets of depths of his short life. It is his journey. My position is as steady witness.

The objects at the edges of this room are plentiful: a dollhouse, an easel, my desk, three grown-up chairs, two child chairs, a trash can, a box of Legos, a container of Lincoln Logs, a sandbox, a milk crate with files in it, a hamper in the shape of a frog (holding puppets and also bedsheets for possible fort-making or covering things up), and a red-yellow-green set of three drawers, one on top of another. The boy pulls each of these objects away from the wall, occasionally asks for help with the heavier things, and makes a neat little path around the perimeter of the room. With few words and sparse instruction he asks that I tack two bedsheets, here and there, over the top of the path to create parts that are like tunnels. "There!" he says at last with a dramatic wipe of his brow. "My secret passage is finished!"

This type of metaphor is what I live for in my working life. They please me, these childhood metaphors that I don't have to pick out of mud and rinse underneath a stream of running hot water before they become clear. A secret passage, indeed. This boy and I have traveled this passage before, and it has led us to the darkest parts of his five years, places no child should ever have to go, including police stations and courtrooms. I predict that today it will lead us into new territory. (If I could only be so clear with my own therapist, my treatment would have ended at least five years ago, maybe even six or seven).

The boy then rummages through a board game and produces a timer, the kind in the shape of an hourglass with sand inside. He lets the sand drain completely from one end to the other and says, "Time to start." Like an excited puppy, the boy drops to his hands and knees and orders me to do the same, behind him. He still holds the timer awkwardly in one hand. Down on my hands and knees I go. "Now, follow me!" he says. And we start. Around the path. Again and again. Like rats in some sort of strange psychological experiment, we circle round and round the secret passage. I begin to salivate.

With each circle, the boy checks the timer. "We still have more time!" he says with each and every pass. This indicates to me that we will circle again, anew. Though the boy begins this race ahead of me by his instruction and I follow the bottoms of his sneakers, soon he is behind me, out-lapping me by one time around. I feel him hot on my tail, nipping against the bottoms of my boots. "Come on! Go faster!" he orders.

My hips catch at the edges of the frog hamper, the Lincoln Logs, and the easel. I am slow. I knock over the Legos with my shoulder while trying to make a corner and they cascade in an avalanche of plastic. Around and around we go, and I do not fit. I am a June bug trapped in an ant farm. Around and around. My wrists ache, my knees burn, my shoes scuff. Around and around. I am a marble stuck in the nostril of a preschooler.

Breathlessly I say to the boy, "So, I need to take a little break because I am much, much older than you and cannot go around so fast. This is very, very hard for older people." I offer that in explanation, though he has not asked for one. I hope to evoke empathy or even pity from him, something I have never, ever had the need to use my age to do, before this very moment. The boy sits in place and watches the sand move from one part of the timer to the other. He flips it over so that the sand begins again; I sit up, rub at my elbows, and catch my breath. I sweat. And wonder when, just when, did crawling become so agonizing. I remember being able to do it well. And indeed, his short journey (our short journey) has drained me of energy.

"We still have more time!" he calls to me and shakes the timer above his head like a dueling sword. "You can take the shortcut over to where I am so that you are behind me again!"

On hands and knees, I cut across the midsection of the room, feeling guilty (I should not desire to evoke pity from my clients, should I?), and take my place behind him once more. He begins to scamper and I follow. Soon he is ahead again, outpaces me by half a lap, and slows to let me catch up.

"Another break," I tell him, feeling wrist bone grind against hand bone. I feel this, but tell him I've stopped to pick up the Legos.

"Cleanup is very important," I say. "Let this be a lesson to you."

We begin the chase again at his insistence, and again he out-laps me by nearly three-quarters. He stops and sighs, and so I stop. I am relieved. The boy, wide-eyed, peers from behind a chair to see me sitting in a tight squeeze between the wall and the frog hamper. My knees are as close to my chin as they can get and splayed to each side. My face is red. I cannot keep up with him.

"Come on you old cow!" the boy shouts out then, more than a hint of frustration in his voice. Come on you old cow. I hear the phrase ring in the corners of my mind. Come on you old cow. And, in those five small words, I know what I have become somewhere along the way: bovine, Bessie, Jersey Girl. And I feel the truth of this rise up from my hooves.

I do not take offense at these five words that on another day could make me cry and vow to never again eat another potato chip. Come on you old cow. True. I taste the remnants of a grassy lunch and my udders drag on the floor.

Suddenly, I am out to pasture, a big gold bell around my neck. I am in a commercial with a pretty blonde girl, selling farm-fresh milk and cheese. I am at a farm show watching competing cows being draped in blue ribbons. My hips sway, my big brown eyes stare off into the distance, and then I moo. Really, what other choice was there? From the depths of my soul, I moo. This moo begins meekly and builds in strength as I go. It is a crescendo of a moo that I will perform only for children or other cows, so don't even think about asking me to replicate it when you see me. But I will tell you, it is a quicker "m" and a long-drawn-out vowel sound. It is a real moo straight from my depths, winding its way around a secret passageway to find the ears of the little boy waiting for me to follow him.

Conscientious Objector

At not quite three years of age, she's the youngest of my clients. The others have graduated to full school days without naps and no need to wear Pull-Ups at night. The top of her head reaches just over the top of my desk. She's not tall enough that I could ask her to flip on the light switch in my office. In width, she is the size of one of the watering cans on the potting bench in my garage. She has curly black hair, blue eyes, and wants desperately to be a ballerina when she grows up. With the secretary in the waiting room looking on, before our very first meeting, and before each meeting since, she's shown me a series of dancerly spins and jumps.

"I am called a therapist. My job," I tell her, "is to help children feel a little better about sad or scary things." She tells me immediately about a bad dream she has recently had.

"Candy corns were falling from up there." She points to the ceiling.

"Goodness," I say. "Falling from way up there . . . and then what happened?"

"That's all," she says, pulling the sandbox from beneath a chair. I imagine swarms of candy corn coming from the sky like locusts, pelting heads, windshields, making highway travel impossible. Twenty-four-hour news broadcasts about this saccharine bombing from an unknown enemy. A candy terrorist.

Then, suddenly, in the presence of this small being, I find myself flooded by thoughts about the broader political situation. The reasons for her being here with me have nothing and everything to do with her. We are at war, and I am not proud of my country on this matter. I wish that those who made the decision to do this, start this whole thing, before she was born, could be here with her and truthfully answer her questions. But my own thoughts are not what's most important. I need to be where she is and respond to whatever she will say. I can't stop asking, "How will she work this out?" I need to quiet my pesky mind that nips at its own edges like a little dog.

My ballerina girl sits down next to the sandbox and hands me a red cup filled with sand. "Coffee for you," she says, "because you have been home with me all day." She then makes a cup for herself.

"Coffee for the both of us home all day," I say. I slurp at the edge of the cup and dump little bits back in the sandbox at regular drinking intervals. Caffeine will help us both, I think, after a long day.

"My daddy," she says, and sips at the edge of her cup— as though we are two old friends, together at a café for tea.

"Your daddy is leaving on Sunday," I say back to her and sip at the edge of my cup. She nods her head and pours dusty sand out of her cup, then from one hand to another. The sand is desert dry and clouds up the space between us. I ask, "Do you know where he is going?"

"Yes," she says, "to Hi-raq." She pronounces the name of the country as if it begins with the letter H. I don't correct her. This is how her young ears have heard the word and made sense of the syllables.

"Yes," I say back to her, "Hi-raq. On Sunday." And then I pose to her an impossible question. "Why is he going there?"

"I don't know," she says and shrugs her shoulders.

"It is hard to know," I say. And though she does not ask me for an explanation, I feel a sudden urgency to give her one. I say, "He will go there to do his job."

This ballerina's father will be deployed in three days. He is an army police officer. He will be gone for a year and will patrol with the Iraqi police. When he returns she will be nearly four. He will have missed a quarter of her lifetime. In my life, at my age, an equivalent absence would mean more than ten years without someone most important. Her father will miss several dance recitals, possibly more than one bad candy corn dream, and three hundred sixty-five bedtime stories. When her father returns, she will be taller than my desk and wider than my watering cans. How am I to help her understand this? Me, the pacifist.

I hate war. I hate this war.

My ballerina girl has been brought to me "just in case." Just in case she has feelings about this, just in case she does not understand, just in case of the worst case possible. And right then and there in her therapy session, I bow my head in silent prayer. In that moment, it is the thing that I am able to do.

The girl stands and draws a large purple face on the dry-erase board. She slowly and carefully forms the eyes and short whiskers of hair on the very top of the head.

"He has short hair," she says. I imagine her father leaning way over to allow his daughter to run her hands over his closely cropped hair. The purple face smiles out at us.

The girl rummages in a drawer of toys. She returns to the sandbox with a plastic superhero doll. He is dressed in a red suit and cape and has a lever on his back that controls his arms in punching motions, back and forth, back and forth. She places him on his back in the sandbox and slowly covers his body with sand. She asks me to help her cover the arms. I pour sand over his fists and then pat it down as I had seen her do. "All gone," she says when he has disappeared.

"All gone," I say. I feel panicked. This ballerina girl seems able to sit with this, but I am not. I think what is most feared. At least by me. What if he dies there? *Unnecessary*, I think. Her father is actually still here. This gives me some comfort. He is sitting in the waiting room. I try to remember from my studies when it is that a person is supposed to understand the permanence of objects: that when something or someone is not right in front of you, it or they have not necessarily disappeared forever. At age one? Two? Ten? Forty?

Generally my rule is to follow a child's story to its own end. The child's end. Not an end created by me for my own sense of security and comfort, even if that end is not what I might expect or want for any child. Children are often much more tolerant of the wide range of human experiences than are the adults around them. They take stories to ends, bitter or fairy tale.

But on this day, because of my panic, I say to her, "We can't see him, but do you know that this man is still under there? Under all that sand?"

"Nope," she says, "all gone. Far away."

I say, "Let's dig and see if he is still under there, even when we can't see him and he is far away." We paw at the sand like cats. She squeals at the sight of a fist. And then a foot. And then his head.

In retrospect, I wonder what would have happened if instead I had said back to her, "All gone! What happens next?" I know the answer, of course. Our time together would have remained about her, not about me.

"There he is!" she says and pulls him out of the ground.

"There he is!" I say. "Even though we couldn't see him for a while and he was far away in Hi-raq, he was still there." I hope this will be true.

She repeats this burial and discovery four more times, each time pulling this superhero from the sand with greater abandon. In and out of the ground goes the man, and a sandstorm swirls between the two of us and we move back to war. Suddenly, in my mind, we are standing together in the dry Hi-raqi desert, candy corn bombs dropping from high places. We dodge white-hot candy tips and breathe dry air into our lungs. I look at my ballerina's shoulders for armor, at her head for a helmet, hoping to see something that might buffer all of it.

I look over at her. She is crying. "Sand in my eye," she says, and I hold her small face in my hands. She points to her right eye, tearing, pinking up.

"Sand in your eye," I say. I pull on her eyelids, first the upper, and then the lower.

"Look this way," I instruct. Her deep blue orb, like a tiny planet, strains to the right.

"Now the other way." I watch the planet at it moves across the milky atmosphere and I think I can see Massachusetts right there, and Hi-raq right over there. I don't see any sand. "Blink three times," I say, "and your eye will feel all better." And suddenly, the blue planet disappears three quick times.

"It is hard to think about Daddies going far away," I say.

"How is your eye now?"

"Better," she says. "No more sand."

"It is time to go," I say, "we are finished for today."

We walk out to the waiting room where her father is waiting for her. "You will be in my thoughts," I say to him. "Thank you," he says. We shake hands. His hand is sweaty, or maybe mine is. I move again into prayer. The little girl shows me a leap and a twirl and they walk out the door together, hand in hand.

Excavator

This six-year-old boy is an eager dentist, with the fervor of a dental student who anticipates the high-pitched whir of the drill, shaves the dark edges of decay to a smooth white-yellow. Dentists make it go away, the place of decay that threatens the body of the tooth. Then they pack the place with silver or porcelain.

To me, a new-fangled dentist once said, "Alice, you will never be able to tell you even had a cavity there." I was forty when she made this pronouncement from behind her blue mask as I gripped the handles of the dental chair with white knuckles. Even now, when I open my mouth wide enough to catch in a mirror a glimpse of my molars, that filled tooth looks whole and white and reminds me of being a child with no worries about shots of Novocain and flossing in the darkness of crevices.

It must be satisfying for a dentist to know that much of what ails a tooth can be fixed and patched, pulled or rooted out, and the tooth's owner sent on his or her way after the appointment. This is how I mistakenly envisioned my work at the beginning; that healing from trauma and loss had the potential of smooth edges and silver linings. But there are no emotional fillings, silver or otherwise. I've since changed my expectations.

When I pick the boy up from his aunt in the waiting room and give a nod, it is as if I've released a metal starting gate that held back a wild horse. The boy runs down the hallway to my office. I can see the bottoms of his sneakers with each step, and he would kick up dust if any were available. He came to me having already been diagnosed with Bottle Rot and Failure to Thrive, as if these were failures on the part of the boy. The adults in charge were the ones who left the binky in his mouth until the small pearls of snowball white baby teeth turned brown, and left him in his crib for long hours without human contact. At six he is the size of a small four-year-old.

Sometimes, when the boy runs ahead of me, I call him back to our starting place. It is what the respectable therapists do. I say something respectable to him. Something therapeutic. Particularly if colleagues are around and give me sideways glances as if to say, "Well, do something, Alice."

"We use walking feet in the hallway," I say. We practice,

starting right then, some sort of containment, holding back the animal urges, the forbidden id. We practice for some faraway position he will take among respectable adults. Secretly, I enjoy the charge of this snuffing bull of a boy, a ring in his nose, his horns pointed forward, and I wish I would charge at things that bring me joy.

This place of doing what I should, ordering him back to his starting place, slowing his feet, is my place. His place was in a crib, left for hours unattended, a bottle of sugar-juice coating the beginnings of his baby teeth. There is a gap between our places, and it is our job to go to that gap together. We visit in the ways he shows me.

The boy slams my door open. It bangs against the opposing wall, shakes a calendar and tilts a picture frame. That surely startles my neighbor. The boy smiles, and for a second, shows me the cave of his mouth. He has no teeth of his own now. Only some carefully fashioned by someone else. Perfect metal, hooked to perfect molds. He takes up a medical bag and orders me to the floor. I sleep until awakened by the jolting crashing of his cymbals. "Time to wake up!"

I stretch and rise. I rub my eyes.

"Time for your appointment!" he says and begins to rummage through the black bag with clasp handles. He plays this every time. I take my place on the preschool-sized chair, in front of him, my knees closer to my shoulders than to the floor.

"Open up!" he orders. And I do. I open my mouth.

I know. I know. I should scrounge up a doll or stuffed animal and offer that instead. Maybe a puppet. And say, "Now, let's pretend I'm this doll and I'm opening my mouth."

I glimpse his fingernails. They have, underneath, the kindergarten day. Play-Doh, I think. Maybe sand from recess. I can't think much more. I tilt my head back.

His dental mirror is a toy; it is made with round, bulky edges, meant to survive the hands of the young. The mirror is some version of tinfoil. And, suddenly, there it is, examining my teeth from the inside. "Uh huh," the boy says. And, "Hmmmm."

"Doc?" I say. "What's the problem?"

He sighs audibly and notices the chip on my left front tooth. "I bit into an almond," I tell him and wonder if I am a respectable therapist. (What if my boss walks in?) The mirror bumps and nudges its way past my canines, back to my molars. The boy peers intently.

"Yup, you have a lot of hurt back there!" He diagnoses me.

The mirror slides against my crowns, two of them, connected by a bridge, a fake tooth, dyed to the color of my others. The mold, I remember, had pleased my dentist. She was proud of her artistry. The reason for the crown was a failed root canal.

My dentist boy sees my fillings, the first of which was made when I was twenty-five and had given up flossing for a while. He sees gum recession and bits of lettuce from lunch. He sees the tonsils I should have had removed when I was five, and stains from twenty-four years of coffee drinking.

The boy sees the fields of pink where my wisdom teeth resided only several years ago, on their sides. Impacted was the official word. All four were pulled on the same dreary morning. I was stuffed with gauze and sent home to worry about dry socket.

"Yes," says the boy, "lots of hurt. It is time for the medicine." He removes a small purple container of soapy liquid from the medical bag and pops off the lid. He removes the wand, dips it around, and blows bubbles in my direction, at close range. I feel his breath on my cheeks. I wonder for a moment about germs. The bubbles float in front of me, around my face, and they land on my lips, nose, and eyebrows. He places a Band-Aid on my wrist. I am better now. No more hurt.

"Now, I will go to the dentist," he says. We switch chairs. I take his information, his name, and the nature of the problem.

"My teeth hurt," he says.

"Okay," I say, "let me take a look." I go in. I go into the place of the gap between us. I see the expanse of his gums, the metal hooks, and the not-real teeth that now help him chew his food.

"I see," I say. "Yes, I definitely see the hurt places. Lots and lots of them." Because isn't this what we do? Dentists and therapists alike? We go to the decayed and chipped places.

I stay in for a while longer, move the mirror this way and that.

"Uh huh," I say. "Hmmmm."

Then, I see the hope. I see the tiny iceberg tips on his bottom gum. The tips that will emerge into strong, sharp, icy mountains. They are there, just below the surface, and they are strong.

"Okay, time for the medicine." I blow bubbles around his face.

He bites like a puppy at some of them. I place a Band-Aid on his wrist.

"All better," I say.

"All better," he says.

Blue Butterfly Open

This is a story about two photographs, both of butterflies. What you need to know about the first photograph is that it was never an actual photograph, although I wished it so. What you need to know about the second photograph is that it is not from my camera, and it was just as it should have been, to my surprise. It was given to me by a young boy.

This is also a story about the power of the inexplicable connections between people. When a connection happens, the space between two people holds the most vulnerable pieces of each, revealed or not, like the inside wings of a blue butterfly rarely at rest for very long. These vulnerable pieces fly and land and reveal themselves and then close back up as camouflage to the rest of the world. To experience these revealing moments with a child client (or with anyone) is pure magic.

What you need to know about the first photograph in this story is that it was never a photograph to my liking. One winter many years ago my father drove the several hundred miles from his home to mine. He does not visit often, and this time, this visit, I took him to a butterfly sanctuary, a place popular with both locals and tourists. The balmy warmth of the butterfly jungle would be a relief from the sharp sting of cold air, I thought.

Butterflies exist in all forms at this sanctuary, from tightly wound cocoons, to babies with wet wings, to elders with frayed edges creeping their way along the branches of trees or bushes. My father and I, along with the other visitors, were cautioned to walk carefully among the butterflies, to step slowly and with awareness, for some butterflies like to walk on their small points of toes across the concrete path without looking both ways. Butterflies can be careless in this way, either oblivious to oncoming traffic or quietly defiant of it.

One of the primary reasons that many people come to the butterfly sanctuary is to take photographs. Some people smear a dab of molasses on the inside of their wrists, or pocket bits of brown sugar before coming in, all in the hopes of becoming butterfly magnets, of sending their sugary scents radiating out. Then, when someone photographs them—smiling, holding a butterfly on one finger or on an eyelash or on a nose—they can show the photo at the office, and brag, "I just have a way with beautiful insects. I guess you could call me a butterfly whisperer."

Although my father and I did not dab our wrists with molasses, I admit that I did lick several of my fingers and hold my hand aloft in the hopes that my lunch remnants (a turkey sandwich on white with a cranberry spread) would look and smell appetizing to at least one winged friend. When this tactic did not work, we used logic. We stood as still as small trees, arms outstretched like branches, hoping butterflies would mistake us for a nesting place. And yet, as still as we were able to stand, butterflies did not come to us. We tried again. Perhaps if we stood in a spot among a flock of butterflies (thousands of them), one would land. When this did not happen, we stood in an empty spot, hoping, hoping we would soon be surrounded. They teased us, those butterflies. They came close, tickled with tips of wings, though none did land.

Of the butterflies that did not land on us that day, one kind in particular caught my eye. A butterfly with two-toned wings: muddy brown on the outside, so that when perched on a limb, with its wings closed together, it blended with the trunk of a tree, or the dirt on the ground, and blue when spread in flight or even briefly at rest, the color of the clearest of oceans. A blue so bright, it was like a streak of aquamarine from a small metal tube of paint. A sanctuary employee whose name pin read "Flight Attendant" told us the outside brown was camouflage.

"It enables the survival of the species, foils their prey," she said.

My father pulled his camera from the pocket of his jacket. He snapped pictures of white butterflies, orange striped, red with black edges. I asked my father for a photograph of the blue kind, with wings open. Either in flight or at rest, I said. I was not particular. I just wanted that blue. He held up his camera and waited, waited for one to soar by and slow down. To sit on a leaf, wings spread. My father took pictures of those blue butterflies, picture after picture. He grunted, sweat, and swore under his breath when each and every photograph seemed snapped a moment too late, and each and every butterfly had closed up its wings. I directed him this way and that. I tried to snap a few frames myself. But we left the sanctuary that day with a photograph only of brown wing against brown tree trunk. A picture of a muddy field and us, tired from chasing. This was the first photograph in this story of two.

What you need to know about the second photograph is that I did not tell any of the children I worked with at the time about my trip to the butterfly sanctuary, nor about my yearning for a photograph of the blue butterfly.

One of the children I met with at that time was a young boy. Though this was many years ago, in my memory it is as though it is now. When I ask him about his age he holds up three fingers, spread wide, and carefully keeps his thumb tucked into his palm. He asks me if I am three also, and I tell him that I am not, though I remember being three and climbing on jungle gyms. And I do remember nursery school, Play-Doh, saddle shoes, and dipping graham crackers in milk cartons for midmorning snack, slurping on fingers to get every last drop.

I sit on the floor when I talk with this boy, and even then he is taller than me by only an inch or so, standing on his Superman sneakers that blink red lights at the heels when he takes each step. Sometimes he wears a white baseball cap, and at other times, a yellow Sponge-Bob watch, though he cannot tell time. We play together when he visits and I watch for small twitches, called tics, around his eyes. Sometimes it looks like he is winking. The secretary in my office giggles when she sees this, thinking he is winking just at her, flirting. She winks back and calls him "a charmer, a real charmer, that one." But these are why he is here. His eye tics. They do not have a physical cause, his doctor has said, but probably result from stress of some kind. His mother has brought him to me to find the cause of his stress. "He is three," she says. "He shouldn't be stressed about anything."

We play together when he visits, often in the sandbox, sometimes with little toy cars. He dumps out a container of Legos, a cascade of red, yellow, and green, and laughs at the loud noise they make falling to the ground. He dumps out Tinkertoys in the same way and covers his mouth, giggles.

"I hear you making your noise," I say.

He laughs again. He buries these toys in the sand. Covers them up, uncovers them by brushing sand with his hands, covers them again.

"It is hard to know," I say, "whether to keep things covered up or to let them be seen."

His eyes open and close, uncover and cover, in quick succession. We play like this for three more weeks, covering and uncovering Legos, toy cars, blocks. We brush and blow sand dangerously close to our eyes. His tics get worse. And then once, when we had not seen each other in several days, from his seat in a shopping cart he asks his mother in a serious way if he can come to therapy again soon, his eyes wide, not blinking.

"I want to go see Alice," he says.

She calls me and I agree to see him the next day.

He enters the office in light brown pants and a Spider-Man shirt. He is wearing his watch. It is time. He is ready. He begins to tell me a story of a game he was taught to play on weekends when he visited with his father. A game played in secret with a father who should have known better and should have never, never played it. It is a game about power, the kind of power taken from one person's most private body by another. It is sexual abuse. It is something the boy does not understand, though he knew to keep it covered up, under sand, under flitting eyelids.

"Will he say 'sorry' to me for playing this game?" the boy asks.

"I don't know," I say. "But he did something very wrong and you need him to feel very sorry about it." I am nodding while I say this.

The boy nods back and picks up a doll from a doll-house family. He throws this doll against the wall with a crash.

"Bad daddy!!" he yells.

"Daddy did something bad," I affirm. He throws the daddy doll three more times (one for each year?) and I say, "I hear your Daddy crashing."

The boy looks quickly over one shoulder as if he has been caught off guard. His eyes blink fast.

He says, "It smells dirty in here."

"Dirty," I say back to him. I am aware that we are there, in that moment, in the past. We are in his past, with his father. Without his father being in the room. It is what is called a flashback. I want to get the boy back to me, back to the present. With me.

Then this boy in the Spider-Man shirt and blinking shoes says my name, and "I'm peeing! I'm *peeing right here.*"

He says this as a warning, urgently. It is a warning for me to do *something* to stop it, quickly. I stay still and sit and watch as dark brown rivers make their way from the zipper to the cuffs of his light brown pants. I think of levees giving way, dams bursting in cinematic slow motion. I cannot stop these rivers and I imagine them, blue with white foam, rushing and roaring over rock. They curve and bend over thighs, knees, Superman sneakers and onto the floor in a clear puddle around his small feet.

I imagine the rivers warm at first against his skin, but then cold like ice, and I say to him, "It is okay that you peed. It was just an accident and you were scared."

I touch his arms gently. My eyes meet his and I will him back into the room.

We call his mother into the office and she carries him to the bathroom. Our time on this day is finished. I make the calls I have to make. Then, I cry blue river tears for him on my way home in the night, wanting to build the strongest of dams with the reddest of brick for both of us.

What you need to know about the second photograph is that this boy returned the following week. He came shyly into the office following his mother, who held a clear plastic bag in her hand, the kind of bag that seals on the top, blue on one side, yellow on the other, combined when sealed to make green. She tells me that she has taken the boy to the butterfly sanctuary since our last appointment.

He took pictures there," she says. "And he *insisted*

that we bring this picture to you. He would not let me leave the house without it today."

She hands me the clear plastic bag with the green seal. Inside is a photograph, protected in plastic, of a blue butterfly on a leaf, wings open, a paint-blue splash of color. A blue butterfly open. With brilliant, brave blue from the inside, out.

Moving from Silence

A silent boy taught me that sometimes I have no idea what I'm talking about. The boy taught me that when I throw big words around, like "systematic desensitization" and "cognitive distortion," I might be the only one in the room who thinks big words are a good idea.

By just being there with me, the boy reminded me that when I was a child I too was nearly silent in school. My voice only fully arrived much later, on some day well into my thirties.

"She is a bright student, if only she would contribute to class," my teachers would tell my mother during parent-teacher conferences. I hid in back rows and counted the heads of those students due to read aloud before me. Then I counted the paragraphs, the sentences in the book. Checked them off in my head and practiced my reading part over and over before it was my turn to go. With a trembling voice and a heat in my cheeks, I read quickly and prayed to some spirit of silence that I would not be asked to recall the words. They disappeared in a swirl as quickly as I had spoken them.

The boy, by his presence, reminded me that teachers generally don't like it when children don't read aloud, especially when you are eight years old and in the third grade. And he reminded me that though time had moved forward for me and my voice is here with me now, there are still children who can't find theirs.

The boy taught me that sometimes a voice comes when it is damn well ready, therapist or no therapist; that a voice can be born from what we think of as tragic and horrible and the-worst-thing-to-ever-happen.

His parents, a concerned mother and father, sat before me. "He doesn't read aloud in school. His teachers can't grade him."

I listened to their story, leaned back in my chair and waxed poetic about anxiety *this*, coping skills *that*, breathing, desensitizing, counting, thinking, and tapping. They nodded expectantly and agreed to bring their son back to my office so that he would read aloud to his teacher. That was our task. I penciled him into the day planner, wrote up his intake, and gave him a diagnosis, a number from the biggest book I own.

On the day of his first appointment, he walked on quiet feet into my office and sat down in a blue chair. I introduced myself, asked him if he knew why he was coming to see me (he shook his head), and spoke about the ways in which I could help him be much more comfortable reading aloud in school. I sat back and awaited his response. His chocolate milk eyes looked at me in a way that reminded me of my puppy. We stared at each other until I began to squirm.

"So, what do you think about all that?" It was my standard question of children in that chair.

I expected him to say, "That sounds like a good plan, Alice."

The boy taught me that sometimes sleeping through a therapy session is just what needs to be done. That is what he did. He curled right around himself like a cat on the seat of that blue chair, tucked his head under an arm, and fell right off to sleep. No discussion, no wind-down, no yawning. Just sleep.

I looked at my clock. Forty-seven more minutes to go. I rubbed at my forehead and pinched my eyes shut for the count of five. I moved to wake him, thought better of it, and sat back. The seconds ticked away slowly into five, nine, twelve, twenty-three, thirty-one, thirty five, forty-two, forty-five minutes. What was I supposed to do with this? I thought of groceries, dentist appointments, haircuts, television shows, old friends, old lovers, and graduate school. At minute forty-seven, I poked at his shoulder. Said his name. He woke with a bewildered look, rose from the chair, and left the office to meet his parents.

His parents were eager. They said his name expectantly and then said, "How did it go?" The boy looked at me. The parents looked at me.

"Fine," I said. "Just fine. He did exactly what needed to be done."

His father, a hearty man and a fan of baseball, clapped him on the back like he had just knocked one out of the park. And maybe he had. The boy smiled.

The boy taught me that sometimes things don't go as planned.

At the second session I did not have time for the fanfare of therapy-speak. He fell asleep immediately, curled in his tight swirl on the seat of the blue chair. His sneakers hung over the side. The soles were red.

Shit. I said this aloud, nearly inaudibly.

I turned to my computer, searched the Internet.

"What to do if your client sleeps in therapy." Nothing. The help was only for sleepy therapists who tend to doze off during sessions right after lunch. At the end of fifty minutes, I poked at his shoulder, said his name, and again he awoke, bewildered.

His mother walked him out of the office.

"I think I might have fallen asleep." He said this to her. It was the first time I had heard his voice. She put her arm around his shoulder.

The boy taught me to return to what I knew to be true. To be where the child is, not where I think he should be. I consulted a colleague. "Put a blanket on him," she suggested. I did this. For the next six sessions.

To his insurance company, I wrote that we were working on building therapeutic rapport and on relaxation techniques.

To his parents, I said what I knew to be true.

"We have to move at his pace." They nodded.

His father said, "You are the expert." They rose to leave the room.

"You know," his father said, "he likes mascots."

Sports mascots. From professional teams. I knew of one, maybe two, in those early times. And, in the seventh session, as the boy began to curl around on the seat of his blue chair, I took out my colored pencils, an eraser, and a blank sheet of paper and began to draw from memory what I knew. I drew the round belly, the stumpy legs, the bulging eyes, the long, fuzzy green tunnel of the mouth and the shockingly protruding tongue. Though he began to sleep, the boy heard my scratches, rose from his seat, and stood near me to watch. The Phillie Phanatic. The singular mascot from my own childhood on the outskirts of Philadelphia, when Pete Rose in red stripes was recognizable to me.

The boy handed me a green pencil and colored in a red P on the Phanatic's shirt, pushing me slightly out of the way as he did so.

At the end of that hour, I handed the picture to the boy. He smiled, pinched a corner between two fingers, and left the room to join his parents.

"What do you have there?" they asked him. He held up the drawing.

His father clapped me on the back. An old buddy out on the diamond.

Sports mascots. They are the fumbling, spinning, bouncing tricksters of the field, the rink, the diamond. They are all of these things, while silent.

The boy came to see me a week later. He dragged my

easel across the room to his chair, sat down, uncapped a red marker and wrote three letters on the dry-erase board. "WLY."

"W-L-Y," I said this aloud, my first sounds to him in two months.

He looked at me.

"Willy?" I guessed this.

He shook his head nearly imperceptibly. The boy rolled his eyes and pointed to his hat, a blue cap emblazoned with two red socks, white at the heels and toes. The Boston Red Sox. Our home team.

"Wally?" I guessed. The boy nodded.

I pulled the image up on my computer screen. Fuzzy and green. Similar to the Phanatic, but not the same. I sharpened my green pencil and got to work. The boy colored in the legs.

The boy taught me that there are many, many, many sports mascots. Thousands, maybe. In both the major and minor leagues. All sorts of sports, professional, collegiate. Each session, he wrote a name on the easel, in block, elementary-school printing. He often left out the vowels. A triceratops, cardinal, seal, moose, squirrel, falcon; Mr. Met, Mr. Red, Gapper, Southpaw, and, from Hartford-WhalerNation, Pucky.

The boy taught me that whales are difficult to draw, head on, without the drawing looking obscene.

Each one, the boy took home.

"He's hanging them in his room," his mother said.

"We had to hang one over the microwave because it got too crowded," his father said.

Over time, the boy began to talk. An inchworm climbing a mountain. The name of a color here, a correction to one of my drawings there. In the beginning, I nearly startled in my seat to hear a noise in the room that wasn't my pencil against a thin sheet of paper, though I tried to roll with him as though we had been talking for years. His voice had the tone of a choirboy at Christmas, soft and higher than my own.

To the boy's parents, I spoke about anxiety. Told them what it was, what it meant.

"You mean," his father sat forward in his seat, his hands on his knees, "it's not because he just doesn't want to talk or do the work?"

"Well," I said, "he doesn't want to talk because it makes him feel anxious. Just like you don't want to do things that make you nervous. Not talking or not reading is his body's way of protecting itself from feeling that feeling. He freezes up."

His father sat back.

The boy's parents and I talked with his teachers. We modified work, made plans, accommodations, gave him buddies. Years passed. I drew more mascots. More years went by, six in total. The boy asked me to draw Big Papi.

"Big Papi," he printed on my whiteboard.

"Isn't that an actual man?" I asked. The boy nodded. I drew and erased, drew and erased. The boy saw my drawing, smirked, and never asked me to draw another human.

The boy spoke when he wanted, haltingly, at school. Teachers called me each and every year. Concerned. His parents came to each and every session.

And then, as happens in treatment that goes on and on, the boy grew up and grew bored. He could think of no more mascots.

"I think," I said to the boy's parents one day, "that maybe we should take a break. Maybe we have come as far as we are going to."

The boy's father sat forward in his chair and held up a pointer finger.

"Ohhh . . . no. Don't think you are getting off that easy," he said. "We aren't doing this journey without you."

We planned for a session later that summer. The boy's father clapped me on the back.

The boy taught me that sometimes a voice comes when the time is absolutely true and in need of words.

I got the phone call on a Thursday morning two months later. The boy's mother. In halting speech. The boy's father had been killed nearly instantly in the screech of tire against road. Three hours before. Suddenly. Horrifyingly. I fell to my knees, covered my open mouth with my hand. There were no words.

The boy's family reminded me that many of us therapists love our clients. In that moment, I had joined the family as a silent mourner. Because of my role in the family, I could not tell anyone who I had lost, too. The boy's mother met my eyes days later. We both cried. And she told me about the boy. And his voice.

"In the hospital, there was the line of surgeons, nurses, emergency workers," she said. "All in the room where they told me he was gone."

And her boy, you know what he did? He rose from his chair, held out his hand to each and every one of them in that line, and said with a certainty and clarity she had never heard from him before, "Thank you for doing your best to try to save my father."

The boy's voice had arrived, from the depths of profound grief. At its own pace. In its own time. When it was most needed. It arrived.

Truth Telling

Truth telling is the starkest part of my job. It makes me feel naked. And there are times I don't like being naked in the middle of this frozen field, cornstalks brown and bent, now-hardened welts in the ground from past rains. Being naked in this way is uncomfortable at best.

There are other parts of my work that make me feel fully dressed, like a lady about town. I tip my hat to passersby and stroll along while twirling my unnecessary umbrella at my hip. Those parts are the play, the crayons, the paint, the dolls, the puppets, and the games. Those parts are the "he's had a better week" and "she didn't have a nightmare." In those parts of my work, I wear a ruffle at my neck and gloves that reach my elbows.

The naked part of my job is one that nobody teaches or discusses, yet parents and guardians of children most frequently seek from me just this type of help: the telling of a difficult truth. The truth about whatever is happening or has already happened *must* be told. Telling the truth is

imperative, because the child already on some level knows
it. Keeping the truth from a child blindfolds his eyes,
spins him three times, and says, "Pin the tail on the life
you *think* is yours."

Truth telling to children requires their adults to do
some soul-searching; it is not something to be done without careful consideration and understanding of a child's
development and circumstance. It requires us to distinguish
between our own truth and theirs while being mindful of
gaps in our explanations. The imaginations of children are
magical, gap-filling places. A child's made-up truth can be
fantastical and self-blaming.

It can be scary to tell the truth to a child and to bear
witness to the child's immediate responses. Early in my
career, I never anticipated this part. I expected the after-
math. I expected to sit with a child in the days, weeks,
or months following the revelation, but not necessarily
during the telling. In retrospect, it seems obvious that
I would be part of such a process, but I hadn't been called
upon for this in the early part of my professional life, and
I wasn't yet a mother then, with responsibilities to tell
difficult truths to my own son.

Every time I sit with a child and an awful truth must
be told, I tremble. I hold my right hand in my left and

squeeze my fingers to try to keep my body and mind in the room. During truth telling, my mind wants to take flight like a flock of nervous birds. It wants to hover above us on the ceiling and look down as if at a movie. I work to tether it. The truth-telling moment is one without play, crayons, or games. It is unblinking. The children are unblinking. And, each time, my professionalism falls away, and my tears fall.

One morning, I hold the hands of a mother. Her hair is matted on one side. Her eyes are red. We talk about her son.

"This," I say to her, "is what you say to him: Daddy was driving his truck and another truck crashed into him. The crash was so hard and your Daddy's body was so hurt that he died. His body stopped working and moving and feeling. This means he will never come home again."

We do not say "passed on" or "went to sleep."

To the mothers of a daughter: "This is what you say to her: Your mommies kept fighting and yelling at each other and now we don't want to be married anymore. It wasn't okay for us to fight so much in front of you. When two people stop being married, it is called 'divorce.' We will live in two homes and you will have time with each of us."

To all of the children we say: "No, it is not your fault.

No, there is nothing you could have done to stop it. No, it isn't fair. Yes, ask any questions you have and we will do our best to answer them. No, it isn't fair. It isn't fair. We will work hard to keep you safe."

We leave as little room for imagination as possible.

The truth, whatever truth it is, hovers over each child in the same way. I watch it there, just over the head, over the bangs, ponytails, and baseball caps. It is the same each and every time. The child stares, eyes round, at a place in the room, usually just beyond the head of their parent. And I wait for their moment of dawning. This dawning is not beautiful; it is a devastating moment, in which part of the soul of the child changes forever and they reel back from what used to be their truth. From this time, there is always a before and after. And we, the adults, can only say, "This is hard. Really, really hard," and "I am here for you."

A boy of ten sits across from me in my office. He wears the newest of the coolest of sneakers. They have zigzags on the bottoms and along the edges. I have heard about these sneakers from others, as wished-for things.

"My mom," says the boy, "got them for me, but thinks that they will end up in the bottom of my closet." He looks down at them and taps his toes together.

"She thinks you will stop wearing these sneakers you love so much," I say back to him.

"Yeah." He shrugs off the conversation and looks away.

I watch our words tumble from the air between us, break up into their letter parts and hit the ground like hail. An "s" rolls near one of his zigzags, an "h" bumps against my leg and lands near my chair.

The boy wears a hat that comes around and over his ears and ties—if he wants it to—beneath his chin. The hat is red with brown designs that remind me of African drums. We talk about snowboarding and a go-cart and a birthday party. And he suggests, as he almost always does, that we play checkers.

I am not a talented player of checkers, though in my job, I play it often. My aptitude for the game rests stagnantly at several years behind this child's age level. I say to the children I see, without reservation, "You know, I don't just let kids win, like some adults. I play full out." We deal with the results, one way or the other.

The boy and I set up our game. He is red and I am black. He moves. I move. Diagonals and zigzags, like the bottoms of his sneakers. Occasionally, one of us jumps, collects the prize, and cracks our knuckles with a self-satisfied stretch. We each exaggerate this stretch like cartoon characters playing poker at a saloon. He started this cowboy part of our games. I copied.

I jump a double.

"King me," I say and stretch out my arms in front of my body. He flips my checker over on his side of the board. I am winning. It is a rare event.

It is his turn. He slides his checker suddenly in a different direction. He moves horizontally and stacks it on top of another and another. Five in all. I raise my eyebrows in question.

"It's a real move," he says. "It is called The Luke Sky-walker."

I raise my eyebrows again.

He is confident. "It's a real move," he says. "It is in the rules!"

He is emphatic. He takes his stack of checkers and leaps around the board, skipping five or six squares at a time, collecting all of the rest of my checkers in the palm of his other hand.

"Luke Skywalker," I say gently, "you win."

The boy sits back in his chair, cracks his knuckles and sighs. He pulls at the ties of his hat. The earflaps stretch down to the edge of his chin.

He kicks at the leg of the table between us.

"Okay," he says.

"Okay," I say back to him.

"I want to know about it," he says.

"Okay," I say, "what exactly do you want to know?"

I half expect him to say, "My truth. I want to know my truth. Would someone please tell me?"

"I want to know why he is in jail and why I can't see him." The boy slouches in his chair. He rests his head on the backrest and looks up at the ceiling. He asks about his father.

"Okay," I say and I rise to invite his mother in.

She walks into the room, sits stiffly on the edge of a chair and pushes her hair behind her ears.

The boy sits up.

"We will tell you why your father is in jail and why you can't see him," I say to the boy. I imagine him as the real Luke Skywalker and place a lightsaber in his hand. I am aware the lightsaber is more for me than it is for him. I want him to have a sword made from the most powerful of lasers for the receiving of this truth.

His mother and I say the words he needs to hear. They are gritty, harsh, shocking. They are the hardest words you can imagine. I feel as if my brain rocks back and forth in my head. I squeeze my fingers to tether the birds. His mother tugs at her collar.

"You can ask us any questions you need to," his mother says. *She is brave*, I think.

As with all the others before him, his truth hovers for a moment just above the red pompon on his hat. I watch it floating there. The boy sits, unblinking, and I wonder, as I have with all the others, if he has heard what we said. My breath is shallow. I waver for a moment on whether the truth is even necessary. It is a place I return to again and again, a place in which I question my own vehemently held truth about my work with children. I consider softening the edges with lies. Yet, I don't. I have never regretted telling the truth.

The boy, his mother, and I sit in the room with our words hovering silently between us. I watch to see if the letters will split apart and crumble to the ground, but they don't.

His moment of dawning arrives like a wave. He recoils as if punched, slides back down in his chair and pulls taut the ties of his hat. The furry edges encircle his face, cover his eyes, and close in around his nose. His face disappears, and he leaves us for a moment. His before is complete. His after begins.

Listen

There is always a space— a hallway or library. I am hard-pressed to think of another profession in which having confidential meetings in stairwells, hallways, and closets is permissible and even encouraged. Alternatively, the back of a classroom or a noisy cafeteria might be where I must bend my head so that my ear is near to the one speaking. These are typical conditions for sharing the most intimate of conversations in the realm of community mental health. Psychotherapy for the poorest children of our cities and our rural, winding roads happens without fanfare; without grand playrooms, art supplies, leather couches, and sometimes, any privacy at all.

Psychotherapy requires intimacy, privacy, and safety. We therapists are taught to have our own baggage lined up neatly and clearly tagged for our destinations. We are instructed to know where we are from and where we are going and about how this may impact the course of a session and the treatment as a whole.

But sometimes destinations get mixed up. We fly off course or miss the flight altogether. Our baggage bursts a seam or a buckle and remains, embarrassingly, on the luggage turnstile, going around and around, until we claim it. We fly under the radar, over the radar, or right smack into it. We hear whatever we want to hear, what our experiences let us hear, and miss the words placed with emphasis right at our doorstep.

I meet with a girl who reminds me again just how important it is to have open ears and heart. She is eight. We meet in her school library at a table near the non-fiction sections. Classes come and go, teachers stop by to return books.

"Do you listen to Oprah?" the girl asks me eagerly.

I think about this. "Well, actually, I really like *watching* Oprah. She is very inspiring."

I sit back and nod as therapists do, pleased here in the school's open-air library that we have found this point of connection.

"No . . . *Oprah*," she says back to me, and cups her hand around her mouth for emphasis. "Do you *listen* to *Oprah*?"

I wonder if she means do I listen for advice of some

sort from Oprah, something therapeutic, every day at four o'clock.

I nod again and say, "I suppose I do to some extent. I even read her magazine sometimes. Usually, though, I don't make it home in time for the show."

I leave out that my relationship with Oprah over the years has run hot and cold and has been soured lately by the price of objects on her *My Favorite Things* list. My salary will allow only the price of her magazine. I sit back once again.

The girl rolls her eyes. "Oprah! Oprah! Oprah!" she says a bit more loudly. Her cheeks begin to flush, her jaw tightens. My palms start to sweat. The librarian looks up from her desk and puts her finger to her mouth to shush us and I instantly feel shamed by this reprimand. I think of a small boy I once knew who, in a drawing of what he thought Heaven looked like, drew a picture of a television set with Oprah onscreen conducting an interview with Beyoncé. I couldn't argue that this may be true. What *was* it about Oprah, anyway? She was powerful. Memorable. Had made her way against all odds.

I take a breath and remember my training. I say, in an even, calm tone while meeting her eyes in an understanding sort of way, "So what I hear you saying is that you want to know if I *listen*," I cupped my hand to my own ear, "to *Oprah*."

Maybe we are talking in metaphors here.

"Well," I say, "what do *you* think?" It is about her perceptions anyway, isn't it?

The girl puts her head down on the table and groans.

I try to think of any other Oprahs. Surely there are no others. The little girl clenches her fists. I squint as if into fog and say carefully, nearly inaudibly, "Winfrey?"

The girl stands then, opens her mouth and yodels. The sound is small at first and carries with it no words. Up goes her voice and then back down and I am riding a Coney Island roller coaster, holding firmly to the safety bar. She sings toward a full crescendo, one of her arms in the air, the other on her chest. The girl's glorious aria echoes through the stacks of Dr. Seuss, Nancy Drew, and books about reptiles. Puccini would have wept.

Teachers poke their heads from the doorways of classrooms, temporarily distracted from lessons, thinking perhaps that music class must have been renegotiated into the school budget. Children put down their Number Two pencils, momentarily relieved of the task of passing state-mandated proficiency tests. The art teacher, pushing his mobile classroom-on-a-cart, clatters to a stop in the hallway, raises his eyes, and seems to whisper a small prayer.

Suddenly (and finally), I am transported to my college listening lab. On a cold winter evening, I wear bagel-sized headphones and attempt to make sense of *Don Giovanni, La bohème, Otello.* I am momentarily transported to a time in which there was space enough to consider the names of Verdi and Mozart. I am transported back to, and acutely aware of, my access to all things classical. My access, really, to anything I could want to hear, see, or do.

Opera.

I was not then, and am not now, a big fan. No, I don't actually listen to opera.

The librarian stands up, eyebrows scrunched down, and makes her hearty way in our direction. I raise my hand to her as if to say that everything is under control. The girl sits back down, and I understand. Now I hear her.

What swirls around and between us always are our differing experiences, our differing accesses to education and wealth. We might be of different social classes, different races, practice different religions. And thus we have set our expectations. She suspects that I listen to opera. I guess that she could only be referring to Oprah. I hear no other possibilities. I see and hear only what I surmise could be available to her on television after school.

"No," I tell her, "I don't listen to opera."

I name a pop rock radio station that plays most often in my car. She knows the song. She is surprised. And so am I.

him/hymn

Sometimes I am in the dark. Really in the dark. Sometimes children turn out the lights in my office. I tend not to like it when they do this, but can appreciate the metaphor. When the lights go out in my office because a child decides that this is what needs to happen next, I feel anxious. Less secure in my stance, less secure in my footing. It is like the ground under my bottom (because I am most often sitting on the floor) is a little less solid. When I can't see the face of a child, my mind wanders to the possibility of cut foreheads at the razor edges of my desk, or the shivering soul of the boy or girl, huddled in the corner of the room, who can't now see me, and who is separate from my arms, my mind, and any skill or knowledge I might offer. It is a free fall with no tether between us.

At times like this I realize how much I depend on reading faces; I am vigilant to a shadow across an eye, a twitch of a lip, or the slight tilt of a head. I don't ever wear sunglasses because behind dark lenses, I feel disconnected from anything solid.

I try to wait them out, these dark times and others with children. Invariably, the computer screen shifts, headlights from the street outside bump themselves through the window, and the child makes his or her way back to the light switch and turns it on. I scan their faces for what might have just been. A moment I might have missed, as they, perhaps, wanted me to.

When I visit a girl four flights up a zigzagging set of stairs that run the length of the outside back of the brick building, I brace myself for midnight in the living room of her apartment. The steps leave me winded, though I've gotten to know them intimately. There are three cigarette burns on step number five, paint drips on fifteen, and the predictable smell of pot wafting from a window as I approach step twenty-one. The same broken toys outside the same back doors, used diapers wrapped around themselves, the same men eyeing my ID, probably assuming that I am Social Services, there to remove a child from a mother or father. I nod in their directions and count stairs. There are forty of them to her door, not including the landings, where I pause briefly to catch my breath.

Sometimes the door is left open for me, and I nudge it with a knock and some sort of announcement that I've arrived. There are no lights turned on here. I enter through the kitchen and slip my feet across the floor, using the table as my guide to the living room. I can see only shadows, dark and darker. There is only one lamp that I am aware of, and it is off. It is most always off.

The window shades are drawn to nearly the bottom of the sill, letting in only a sliver of afternoon sun. This sliver is the reason I find the sofa. As I write these words, my fingers keep typing "silver," a precious metal. I realize now that this bit of light at the bottom of the window is indeed a precious glittering metal. Without it, there would be total darkness. I sit down, and the girl sits next to me. Her arm brushes mine, and her feet swing out in front of us. I feel the pulse of her legs bouncing the sofa cushions. I put my bag on the floor at my feet.

"I can't let the sun in today." Her mother says this from a chair across the room. "I just can't let the sun in. It hurts my eyes."

The sun hurts her eyes on days like this. I can only imagine that it burns and illuminates the edges of what is real, including a photograph on the wall of a little baby dressed in a yellow jumper. I have seen the photograph on brighter days. On those days, the baby joins us for our time together. He is also there with us in the dark, when his presence is known to us only out of habit, out of our knowing that he is with us. In the picture, his tiny face shows that vague, fuzzy expression so present in infancy. His eyes can't focus on a distant object and his muscles have not yet learned how to smile.

I am in this room with this family because of a burn that seared through the center of them; it was the accidental death of that infant boy at the hands of the girl by my side. Her brother. She had only wanted to feed him. A single grape. She was four. He was three months old.

"It was an accident." I say this over and over to them each time I visit. It is what I have come to believe needs to be repeated. *It was an accident.* I say this to myself and to them. On this day, the girl rummages in my bag for paper and markers. Even in the dark she knows where they are.

"You can't let the son in, not today," I say back to her mother. Silently, I replace a "u" with an "o" between the "s" and the "n." She doesn't hear me do this. At least, she doesn't know that she hears me, or my thoughts. So much unspoken happens in therapy, a profession known for talking, talking, talking. So much happens under cover, in the darkness of the subconscious, mine and hers.

We sit with the silence in the room, while my mind screams. It screams an image of my own son, not so long out of his own infancy. I am a mother, just out of infancy. He has just started to eat bits of food, cut into tiny pieces. I cut them into crumbs and he paws at them with small hands. Sometimes the pieces find his mouth. At other times, they land on the floor and are licked up by our eager dog. There is a name for this in our profession: countertransference. This is when a therapist's own feelings and old memories are stirred by what their client is doing or saying. Suddenly, my past and present comes into the room. Thinking of the infant boy in the photograph is nearly intolerable for me, now that I have a son of my own.

"The sun is too harsh," she says. "It hurts my eyes."

I look over at the light at the bottom of the window. It is the size of a ruler. Through the sliver, I can see silver light and the bricks from an almost identical building next door, owned by the same landlord, who doesn't allow air conditioners until the middle of July, no matter the temperature.

"It is so hard to look at the son." Again I replace the "u."

I have nothing more to say.

The little girl pulls the cap from a marker and brings

her paper to the light of the window ledge. She begins to draw. Her marker travels the edges of the page. Purple, then blue, then yellow.

"Why?" her mother asks, and I know that she is holding the golden cross around her neck. She has worn it each time I have seen her. Her eyes fill with tears.

"I don't know," I say. This is not a new question, though I'm never quite prepared for its coming. Years of training and practice still leave me without answers for her.

"Why would he do this?" she asks. I wonder if she is talking about her son.

"Who?" I ask. I sense that she pulls at the cross.

"God." Her voice is flat.

Him. Capital H. He. Part and all of the Trinity, her trinity, that includes a Father, Son, and the ghostly image on the wall of a boy who was with her in flesh not so long ago. It is that power of three—used, misused, quoted, understood, misunderstood. Used and misused to both love and hate, and mostly excluded from therapy sessions. We explore the deepest crevices, but often without the acknowledgment that something larger may be present. For some of us, not all.

For this girl's mother, one trinity is the before, during, and after. The joy of the before and the birth of her son, the trauma of the during on that horrible night, and the sharp rays of grief in the after. The other Trinity includes the life of a Son who died while His mother was there. She watched Him die. Her only son. She (they) bore a mother's sorrow I cannot comprehend. Nor can I even go near. It is like getting too close to the sun.

But the Son is here with us now. The ghost of the boy is here, too. Holy. I must trust in this process. Her process, whether or not it is mine.

I shift in my seat to look at the girl's picture. It has the chaos of drawings made by hurt children. Though she is nearly five years old now, she scribbles like a child just learning to hold a crayon. I cannot make out the content. I have come to believe that what it looks like on the paper is often an indication of what it feels like inside the mind and the heart. I place my small, imaginary self at the lower corner of the picture and I feel wind knocking me down, lightning bolts nearing my body, and cold rain pelting my skin.

"You think He did this," I say to her mother. I speak of God. She shrugs, and we suddenly have entered a space usually reserved for others designated to talk about such things. Others who know the stories, repeat the passages, wear the collars. I don't know what to say.

"Do you think God is here?" I ask.

She shrugs again. We fumble. I look around. My eyes have adjusted to the dark. The girl draws and gives me the paper. She points to a circle in the middle of the page. It is him, her brother, her mother's son, central to the storm. I put the picture in my bag.

"I will hold it for you," I tell her. I feel clumsy. I need help with this conversation.

On my next visit up the forty steps, I bring a pastor. A Reverend. To help us. To help me. She takes the stairs with more ease than I do. She breezes in like light, but is dressed in dark, with a white collar. She will answer the questions, I think hopefully. I take in the scent of her shampoo. She smells different from this place. She is not of rice and beans and ammonia.

The shade is up today. The sun is in the room. The silver sun, and the precious son.

With her, we talk about God, the Son, and her son. We ask why and still have no answers. She is expert, this Reverend, in something indefinable. Are there answers? Maybe not. Can we be held in the dark by something light? Maybe. We hold hands and the little girl tells us of a dream of her brother. "He was there in front of me," she says. "He reached up with his hand and moved my hair."

She pushes her bangs gently to the side. The pastor reaches over, places a hand on each cheek and also gently moves her bangs to one side.

"Of course he did," she says. We move then into prayer, our eyes closed. With our eyelids, we shut out the light for a moment, in the hopes that, when we open them, more will come. I squeeze the hand of the little girl and pray.

Wing Against Leaf, Again

Liquid. It is the only state of matter that has definite volume, but no fixed shape. It conforms to the shape of the environment around it, unless the environment is too small or the liquid too big or too active. Then, it spills over stream banks, bursts through dams, and erodes the sands of beaches.

Recently I learned that, on their way to becoming butterflies, caterpillars turn from a solid bug to liquid goo while inside the chrysalis. Enzymes released by the caterpillar consume its solid body. Its body enters this nearly total liquid state; it is a necessary, transformative pause between the before and the after, the past and the future.

I had imagined a much more steady, less dramatic transformation. In third grade, we set up green netting, some sticks, and a few leaves and kept track of caterpillars that had been sent in the mail to our teacher, a strawberry-haired woman who also taught us how to tell time on clocks with hands. In class, we drew our observations of the chrysalis and noted when the butterflies, looking wet and stringy, emerged and dried themselves off. We released them in a ceremonial event on the playground and waved them off to some warmer, more southerly place.

Back then, I had not known that a liquid state was involved, reasoning that if we (my classmates and I) were born of monkeys, then the wings of a butterfly must come directly from the feet of a caterpillar, or some such thing. The head, I thought, stayed mostly the same. In fact, I thought very little about the goings-on inside the dark place. Finding out the truth in middle age makes me wonder what else I don't know. This transformation seems stunning to me and makes me think about how it would feel to melt.

Last week, in a turn of events I could not have predicted, I saw the butterfly boy again and nearly melted. For the first time in many years, he walked through the door to my office. He is in that gawky adolescent stage of life, wears braces on his teeth. He has not yet grown wings with brilliant blue. He is still soggy. But when we saw each other, we embraced. This time, at eye level. His mother joined and hugged us both. We made a little cocoon around this boy, his mother and me, right there in the waiting room, and he held on longer than most thirteen-year-old boys I know would have, I suspect.

The story about how he came to be here with me, ten years from the time we first met each other, is in keeping with him. It surprised me in the moment, but in retrospect maybe it should not have been surprising at all. In preparation for this book of essays, the boy of the butterfly photograph made his way back to me. I had been searching for him, the butterfly boy. And as I did so, the memory of him had come to perch on my shoulder at certain times of day. Sometimes I imagined blue wings fluttering against my cheek, much in the way my son now gives me butterfly kisses with his eyelashes. It is ten years since the butterfly boy brought me that photograph in that clear plastic bag. Ten years since he stood in a puddle of his own making on the floor of my office. In my mind, he still could be any age. Sometimes three. Sometimes seventeen or twenty-five. Was he older than me now? Hasn't he always been?

Ordinarily, I would not be on a search for past clients. It is not something that we are taught is right to do. Our help is time-limited. We journey with our clients for the time that is necessary, hold the memories, the accomplishments, and the horror, and then let go. I suppose that is supposed to protect us all in a way.

I do imagine how my former clients may be faring. I imagine them older, stronger, voices deeper. But I don't go looking. However, I searched for this boy's mother in order to get consent to use the story of her boy in this book.

I tracked old numbers in old appointment books, numbers scratched out, rewritten. I searched the Internet and found matching names across the state. I called one of them.

"You got the wrong number," answered a man, gruffly.

"So sorry," I said, unnerved. Wrong numbers unnerve. I encounter the life of a stranger, uninvited. I quickly exit. I was looking for the familiar.

I tracked down town records and phone books, and I rejected offers from cyber detectives who claim to be able to locate anyone, anywhere for just $9.99 a month. And then, on a Monday morning in early January, a colleague appeared at my door. She apologized, explaining that she had picked up my mail weeks ago, put it in her workbag, and left it there.

"There was something for you," she said, handing me an envelope.

I am breathless. He is there. Suddenly. His mother's name on the return address label. Inside, a holiday card. His photograph on the front. He is a teenager. On the back, in her familiar writing: "He is doing well and would like to come see you again. We've been searching and hope this gets to you." A bright blue wing flutters nearby. And I remember that this work is always, always about connection.

He has asked again to come and see me. Just as he did from the seat of the shopping cart so many years ago. Just as I was trying to find him. "I want to go see Alice." I hear echoes of his voice from years ago. We schedule a session.

It is a Saturday morning when the boy and his mother arrive at my office. I invite them both inside. His mother sits at the edge of the sofa. I also remember her, those many years ago, at the edge of her chair, saying, "He blinks and blinks after visits with his father." We are there in some strange replaying of the past, trying to figure out why. I remember his eyes and their rapid-fire stutter, like the shutter of a camera capturing moment-by-moment still frames of the abuse that brought us together to begin his journey. Today, his eyes are steady.

· We do our paperwork, take signatures, and make a copy of the insurance card. His mother leaves us.

"This is wild," he says. His voice is deep.

"I agree," I say. "You are back. You asked to come back again."

We sit in silence for a moment.

"I want to know your story," he says. He was never one to beat around any bush.

"My story. You mean *your* story?" I ask.

"I guess so," he says.

"You want to remember," I suggest. He slightly nods.

The middle parts of memory are liquid, I think. They are the gooey, enzyme-eaten photographs of the past. They are the color of sepia. These parts of memory are exactly that place between two solids; they are in between the event itself and the meaning they will hold later on. In this liquid place in the chrysalis of memory, there is twisting and turning of images and words, there is making things worse, making things better, or not remembering at all.

Our brains work hard in this transformative place, to let in or to leave out. As from a spigot of a sink, sometimes memory drips, sometimes it floods. The butterfly boy, here with me now, asks for his memory. From me. But really, he wants and needs his own. Doesn't he? My mind rattles with the consequences of just telling him, placing what I've been holding squarely on his shoulders.

"The thing about stories," I say, "is that I can only tell my own. Not yours."

"Oh." The boy sits back on the sofa and then says, "I remember it all."

I think about the rivers down the legs of his pants and the puddle on the floor that I dabbed up with paper towels at the end of the night. I remember the red of the Legos, the slap of the doll against the wall, and the phone calls afterwards. I remember a courthouse and a judge. I remember feeling cold.

"All of it," I say back to him. "Would you like to tell me what you remember?"

The boy thinks. He mentions a cigarette burn, a camera, and photographs that should not have been taken. And then, "The rest is sort of blank. I thought I remembered more. That's what it's been like. Sort of blank."

"You came back to fill in the blanks," I suggest. He nods.

In this moment, and in others, I admire the tenacity of our defenses, those worker bees of the subconscious.

They buzz about inside the mind and place this memory in a drawer and that memory in a safe, make you mad at him instead of her, and cause you to hover like a ghost at the edges of a room, all in the hopes of self-preservation. All efforts toward a brain we can carry around to work or school, in front of friends and family. I admire our defense mechanisms and do not work to break them down. I don't tell this boy what I remember.

I do tell him some of what I know. But only some. He has forgotten about the photograph of the butterfly. He has forgotten about the Legos. He has forgotten that he used to walk into my office with a self-assuredness and swagger that caused our secretary to light up every time she saw him. We put some of his narrative into place.

And I tell him this: "Ever since you were a little boy, you have known just what you have needed to do. You have known exactly when to come and see me. We need to trust your brain again—what it lets you remember, and what it lets you forget. If you tell me that you remember something, I will tell you if I remember it, too."

I ask him, "Does that sound okay to you?"

He says, "Yes, because I trust you." His eyes are unblinking. My breath catches with the weight of his words and the years behind them. We sit in silence for a moment.

"Why didn't he go to jail?" He asks me this with a steady gaze.

I hear him as a boy of three ask again in the liquid of my memory, "Will he say sorry to me?" *Will there be any consequences for him?*

I explain the best I can, but really have no answers that help.

"*Why didn't he go to jail?*" I ask myself.

Memory. In its chrysalis phase it may seem to disappear completely, when it is just awaiting transformation and shifts in meaning and perspective. This boy and I begin our search for his again, like open wing against leaf.

Epilogue

Friends and colleagues who have been my first readers want to know, "How are these children doing today?"

They ask with an urgency I can appreciate. We come to care deeply about these children when we share such intimate moments with them, either in a therapy session or on the pages of a book. I have been in touch recently with most of the families of the children in *Blue Butterfly Open*. Time has passed. Some of these children are now adults. Without exception, they are okay. Some are thriving, some are hanging in there. All are okay.

I hope I can attribute this at least in part to our early therapeutic work together, including with their families. I believe in the importance of this early work, this chance to explore and take the time to make sense of situations overwhelming to them. When we give children the chance to tell their stories, when we recognize how imperative this process can be for their well-being, they readily become our best teachers and guide us in helping them heal.

Acknowledgments

It is with deep gratitude that I acknowledge Carol Edelstein and Robin Barber of Gallery of Readers for supporting years of writing, storytelling, and growing. Thank you for giving me the space and time to become a writer.

I am grateful to the following regular (and encouraging) listeners and readers: Brett Averitt, Mary Beth Caschetta, Meryl Cohn, Don Horton, Susan Cocalis, Joan Cenedella, John Corbett, Ronnie Rom, Linda Barnes-Aaron, Kathie Fiveash, Beth Dirks, Liz George, Pat Stacey, Barbara Lucey, Carolyn McKeown, Brooks Gleason, Bill Barber, and Carolina Clark.

I also want to recognize those who have provided clinical support over the years. This work would not be possible without you. Thank you for challenging and supporting me with humor, pointed questions, and, sometimes, silence and knowing looks. Thank you to Jennifer Brelsford, Joan Groden O'Connell, Virginia Maxson, Ginny Maxwell, Adele Oppenheim, Barbara Weiner Dubek, Annie Rogers, James Levine, Miles Morrissey, Carol Edelstein, Andrea Jontos, Jay Indik,

Christine Edwards, Sarah Mixter, Sarah Rigney, Jane Garcia, and the members of my outpatient and early childhood teams.

Finally, I would like to recognize Bonnie Atkins (who crosses all spheres) and Jesse Sky for their giving of love and time, and the community of the Haydenville Congregational Church for reminding me every week of the bigger picture.

About the author

Alice Barber is a licensed mental health counselor and registered Art Therapist. She has been practicing psychotherapy since 1997 and specializes in the treatment of young children who have experienced trauma. She received her undergraduate degree from Wellesley College, her graduate degree from Springfield College, and a certificate in the practice of Child and Adolescent Psychotherapy from the Smith School for Social Work. Originally from Kennett Square, Pennsylvania, Alice currently lives with her wife, son, and little dog in Western Massachusetts.

In 2011, Gallery of Readers became a 501(c)(3) private nonprofit foundation, with the mission to stimulate interest in, and access to, literature written by emerging creative writers. The foundation promotes educational workshops for writers, develops and offers opportunities to enlarge the audience for their art; publishes books and broadsides; and ensures access to such without restrictions based on gender, orientation, age, education, or income levels; and to perform any other acts necessary to achieving these goals.